SUPER SMART INFORMATION STRATEGIES

MAKE THE GRADE

by Carol A. Gordon

CHERRY LAKE PUBLISHING • ANN ARBOR, MICHIGAN

A NOTE TO PARENTS AND TEACHERS: Please remind your children how to stay safe online before they do the activities in this book.

A NOTE TO KIDS: Always remember your safety comes first!

Published in the United States of America
by Cherry Lake Publishing
Ann Arbor, Michigan
www.cherrylakepublishing.com

Content Adviser: Gail Dickinson, PhD, Associate Professor, Old Dominion University, Norfolk, Virginia

Book design and illustration: The Design Lab

Photo credits: Cover, ©iStockphoto.com/sjlocke; pages 3, 8, 15, and 17, ©iStockphoto.com/bluestocking; page 9, ©Curtis Kautzer, used under license from Shutterstock, Inc.; page 13, ©Thorsten Eckert/Alamy; page 14, ©kristian sekulic, used under license from Shutterstock, Inc.; page 18, ©wow, used under license from Shutterstock, Inc.; page 20, ©Kiselev Andrey Valerevich, used under license from Shutterstock, Inc.; page 25, ©Bill Bachmann/Alamy; page 27, ©Jacek Chabraszewski, used under license from Shutterstock, Inc.

Library of Congress Cataloging-in-Publication Data
Gordon, Carol A.
Super smart information strategies. Make the grade / by Carol A. Gordon.
p. cm.—(Information explorer)
Includes bibliographical references and index.
ISBN-13: 978-1-60279-642-3 (lib. bdg.)
ISBN-13: 978-1-61080-259-8 (pbk.)
1. Activity programs in education—Juvenile literature. 2. Critical thinking—Juvenile literature. 3. Circus—Juvenile literature. I. Title. II. Title: Make the grade.
LB1027.25.G67 2010
372.139—dc22
2009035504

Cherry Lake Publishing would like to acknowledge the work of The Partnership for 21st Century Skills. Please visit *www.21stcenturyskills.org* for more information.

Printed in the United States of America
Corporate Graphics Inc.
July 2011
CLFA09

Table of Contents

CHAPTER ONE

A Juggling Act

The smell of popcorn. The silly music. The amazing sights. There's nothing quite like the circus. Have you ever been to a circus or seen one on television? Think about your favorite parts of a circus. Do you like the lion tamers? Or maybe the clowns? It takes a lot of work to run a circus. There are many different jobs and details to work out.

What does the circus have to do with you or your schoolwork? Being an information seeker is a bit like being a circus performer. You may not be riding a unicycle or blowing fire. But you are learning to do things that can be just as complicated. As a student, you are learning to be an expert at finding, sharing, and presenting information. You juggle different jobs and tools. Pretend you are working on a science fair project. You might need to use the library catalog to find the perfect books for your project. Or turn to a search engine to find good Web sites. Like the tightrope walker, you will have to find a good balance of reliable sources. You'll also have to make informed decisions about which resources to use and which to set aside. The process won't always be easy. You may fall into your net a few times before you become a master information explorer. But luckily, you have the chance to practice and learn from your mistakes.

In this book, you'll learn how to find good information. You'll also figure out how to evaluate your skills through self-assessment. The evaluations that teachers make of your work are very important. The grades they give you are a way to show whether you are on the right track or not. You may really want an A. You may cringe at the idea of getting a C+. So how do you get more A's and fewer C's? Let's learn more about ways to ace school projects. Once you've mastered these challenges, you'll be like an organized ringmaster. Success at school and good grades will be the grand finale of an exciting show!

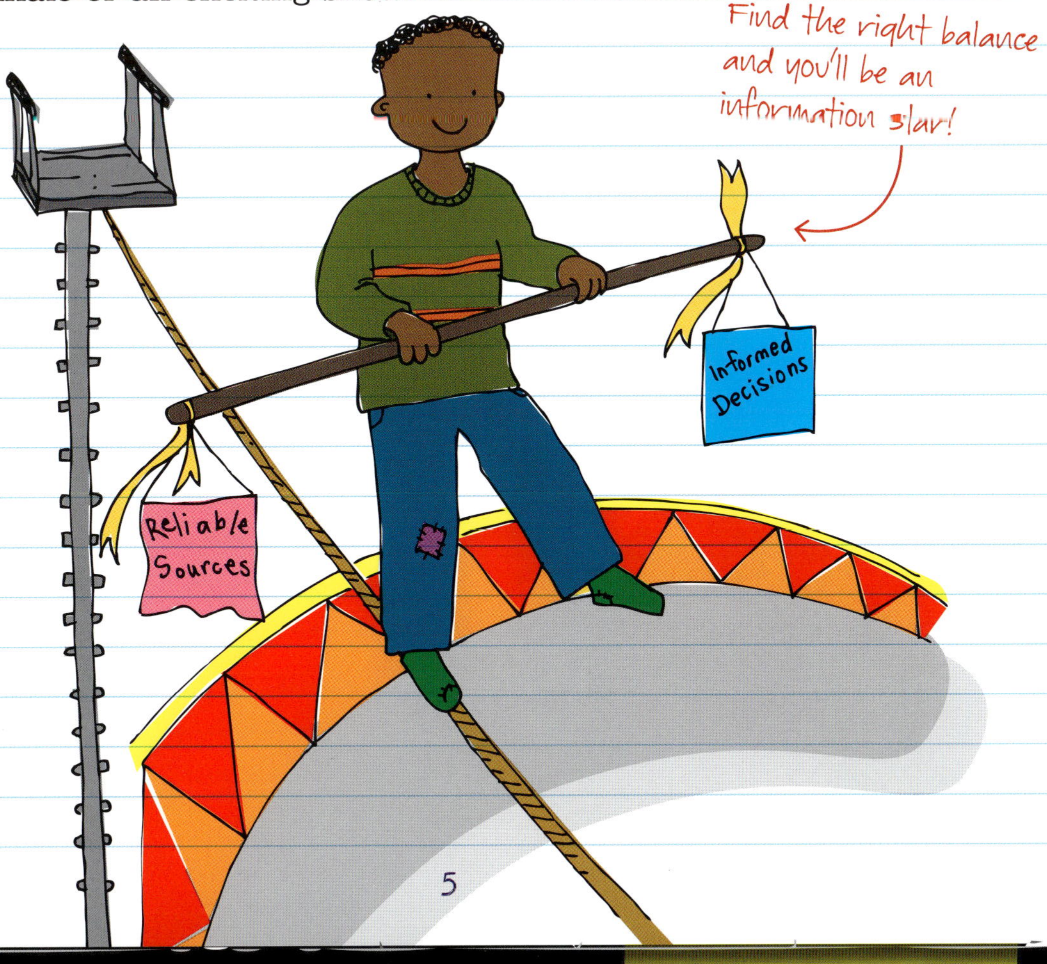

TRY THIS!

A successful research project begins with finding interesting questions to answer. You might know a lot about the circus. But what don't you know? Work with two friends or classmates. Each of you should make a list of five circus topics that you would like to know more about. Maybe you would like to learn about the history of circuses. Or what kinds of animals are used in acts. After everyone is finished, compare lists. Do you all wonder about similar aspects of the circus? Do your friends' notes spark your interest in different aspects?

Now it's time for you to make a decision on your own. Which ideas or topics are you most interested in investigating? Make a new list of two or three circus questions or topics that you would like to research. Focusing the direction of your project is important. It will help keep your research on track.

What resources would you use to research how elephants are trained?

Have you ever thought about what makes a good circus? You may think a great circus needs to meet certain standards. Standards are points or rules that help us decide how good or effective something is. Here are some sample circus standards:

1. The lions perform all of their tricks—and they don't eat the lion tamer!
2. The jugglers don't drop anything.
3. The clowns get a lot of laughs.
4. The audience applauds and cheers at the end of each act.

We should use standards when judging books and Web sites, too. You should use only reliable sources for your projects. You want to be sure the information they provide is correct. For instance, think about what makes a good nonfiction book. Is it the way it looks? Or the information it contains? Or a combination of both? A reliable book is current and written by an expert. It will often have a table of contents and a bibliography. It will also have a glossary and an index. Reliable Web sites are updated often. They may also be managed by universities, government offices, historical societies, or museums. Be careful about using Web sites that have a lot of advertisements. Their main purpose may be to sell you something.

TRY THIS!

Let's practice evaluating a print resource. Look up nonfiction books about circuses in your school library or public library catalog. Choose one book to read and pull it off the shelf. Then rate the book using the rubric below.

QUESTIONS TO ASK YOURSELF	RATING 1=yes 0=no
Does the book contain good information? Can I spot any errors?	
Is the author an expert? Can I find information about the author's life experience or education?	
Is it easy to find information in the book? Are there a table of contents and an index?	
Are there chapter titles or headings that further help me find the information I need?	
Does the book have images that help me understand the text?	
Is the reading level right for someone my age?	

When you are done, add the numbers in this column

Add up your ratings. A perfect score is a 6. The higher the total, the more likely the book will be a good fit for your research.

CHAPTER TWO

The Magic Journal

Practice will help you master any skill you want to learn!

Circus performers work hard every day so that their performances are almost perfect. They learn how to do things that most people can't do. How? Practice, practice, practice! They work on different skills over and over again. They think hard about tricks and ways to improve them. Performers may improve by reading about the tricks, too. They also learn from other experts in the field. Sometimes performers invent their own tricks. Or they tweak the tricks they already know.

Magicians sometimes keep a journal to help them learn tricks. They may write notes. They may also draw or copy pictures in their journals. This can help them remember how to do the magic tricks. When they practice, they might record the mistakes they made or any steps they found difficult. This helps the magicians keep track of what they know and how they can improve.

You can keep a journal for your project, too. Picture your journal as a way of thinking out loud. You don't need fancy supplies to keep a journal. Any pencil and notebook will do. Your teacher may give you writing prompts or guides for your journal entries. The prompts may present specific questions or help you think about your learning.

A journal is a great way to keep track of your progress toward any goal you've set.

TRY THIS!

Grab your magic wand. It's time to become a circus magician! Find books and Web sites that explain how to do magic tricks step-by-step. Choose a magic trick that you would like to learn and perform for a friend. Be sure that you have the supplies you need to do the trick. You will use a journal to track your learning progress.

Follow these steps:

1. Use this writing prompt to help guide your journal entries as you practice the magic trick: Describe the magic trick you want to learn in your own words. Can you find pictures in books or online that demonstrate how to do the trick? If so, photocopy or print them out. Paste them in your journal. As you practice the trick, keep track in your journal of the date and what you did. Concentrate on what you found difficult to do. You may want to ask someone to take photos of your practice sessions. Then you can add them to your journal.
2. Write a new journal entry on at least three different days as you practice your magic trick. Your journal should show the progress you are making. Are you feeling frustrated with a certain step in the trick? Include your feelings and thoughts.

continued →

TRY THIS! (CONTINUED)

3. When you feel ready, show your magic trick to a friend. Then use your journal to share how you overcame any challenges and mastered the trick. Did using a journal help you organize your thoughts and monitor your progress?

Now that you've mastered your magic trick, what else can keeping a journal help you learn?

If you are keeping a project journal on your own, think about sharing it with a teacher. He or she can help you make sense of your entries. Using a journal is a great way to assess your progress in any activity. You can create journal entries to track a research project or science experiment. You can also use a journal to evaluate your study habits. You have many options. So take advantage of this helpful learning tool. It'll bring you one step closer to making the grade.

CHAPTER THREE

Teamwork

The skills needed to work with others will be important in many areas of your life.

Circus performers often work with people from around the world. They all learn from one another. If people did not collaborate, or work together, there would be no circus. All the performers must do their jobs. Many times, they perform in groups. They have to trust one another and work well together.

Do you enjoy working in a group? Learning to work together is an important skill. There will be times when you have to work on group projects. Some group members are natural leaders. But everyone has

Working with others can make projects more fun.

important tasks to perform when working together on a project.

Suppose you are in a group that has to create a poster. The poster will be an advertisement for the circus. As a group, you would need to discuss what the poster should feature. Here is a poster checklist with some things to include:

- An original title for the circus. It should be interesting and make people curious.
- An original drawing that will make people want to come to the circus.
- The date, time, and place of the circus.
- An imaginary telephone number to call for tickets.
- A URL of an imaginary Web site that people can visit for more information.

TRY THIS!

When you begin a group project, it is important to split up the responsibilities. Otherwise, you and your teammates may do the same tasks. Or some tasks may never get done at all! Work in a group of three to four students to create a circus poster. You will need a poster board, markers, and colored pencils.

continued →

Gather your supplies.

TRY THIS! (CONTINUED)

Here are some guidelines to help you divide the work:

- One person comes up with a phone number and URL for the circus.
- One person comes up with a date, time, and place for the circus.
- Everyone uses library resources including books, Web sites, and databases to get ideas for interesting poster art. Everyone should agree on the original image you will create.
- One person draws and colors the picture.
- Everyone brainstorms and decides on a great title for the circus.
- One person writes the text on the poster.

Everyone should agree on who does which tasks. Set a deadline for each step. Observe or keep notes about how well the group worked together.

Your teacher is not the only person who can assess your work. Sometimes students can rate each other. This is especially true after completing a group project. Review the following rubric. It will help you reflect on the poster-making process. The collaboration standards describe three different levels of success for group work. The rating of 1 is not so good; 2 is okay; 3 means the members of the group worked very well together.

HOW DOES MY GROUP RATE?	COLLABORATION STANDARDS
1	One person did most of the work. Many problems were not solved, so the group did not finish its work.
2	The group shared the work, but there were problems in getting the steps done (everyone didn't meet their deadlines, for example).
3	The group shared the work equally. Everyone respected others' opinions. Problems were solved and the group finished its work.

What score do you think your group earned? Did everyone work together? Did some people not take on their share of the work? When you are done assessing your group, step back for a moment. Reflect. What could you have done differently to make your group's work go even more smoothly?

When you take time to assess your work, some important things happen. First, you recognize the mistakes you made. This often keeps you from making the same mistakes again. Second, you realize your strengths and successes. This gives you an opportunity to feel good and to praise your teammates. The process also helps you work better with others in the future.

What are some things you can do to make sure your group works well together?

What if other groups created posters, too? Part of your project may be to assess those other posters. The process of looking over and commenting on another classmate's work is called peer review. During your group assessment activity, you evaluated the process of working with others. During peer review, you evaluate the final product (the poster itself) of your classmates. If you were to review another group's poster, you would consider the poster checklist that you followed when creating the circus ad. You would see if the posters of your classmates include all or most of the points on the checklist. You could also consider the points on the list to the right:

CHECKLIST

- What is good about the poster?
- What questions would you like to ask about the poster? Is anything missing? Is there anything you do not understand?
- What suggestions could you offer to make the poster better?

When you answer peer review questions, share your thoughts with the other groups. Then think about the reviews you received. Talk with your group members. How can you make your poster better? Then you could list the changes you would make based on the peer review comments you have collected.

Part of being an information explorer is respecting the efforts and viewpoints of others. Always offer comments or suggestions about another person's project in a positive way. Do not just say that something doesn't work. Explain why you feel that way and how that aspect could be improved. Word your thoughts carefully.

Chapter Three: Teamwork

Listening to suggestions from others can help make your project the best it can be.

As you work on projects, both by yourself and as a group, you may notice something very important. Successful projects—reports, presentations, experiments, and more—are often edited and revised over and over. Almost nobody gets it right on the first try! So be open to suggestions from your classmates and teachers. Helpful ideas and suggestions come from many different sources.

CHAPTER FOUR

The Show Must Go On

There may be days when a research project is frustrating. Maybe you can't find good Web sites on your topic. Or the library books you need are already checked out. You may not be sure what to do next. Don't give up! There is a phrase that all performers know: The show must go on. You need to keep trying, even if everything seems to be going against you.

Sometimes, you have to change your course of action in the middle of a project. For example, you might not find the information you need. In that case, you'll need to adapt and revise your plan. Being a successful researcher often means being flexible and making changes as needed.

No matter what your age, you'll find that learning is a lifelong process. Some subjects will be easy for you. Others will be more difficult. Think back to a subject or task that you found challenging when you were younger. Maybe you had a hard time memorizing your multiplication tables. Perhaps you found that writing out the math problems over and over helped you memorize them. Thinking about what works and what doesn't work for you as a learner is important. It helps you identify your strengths and pinpoint your limits. Then you can improve your weaknesses. Do you see how self-assessment is a valuable process?

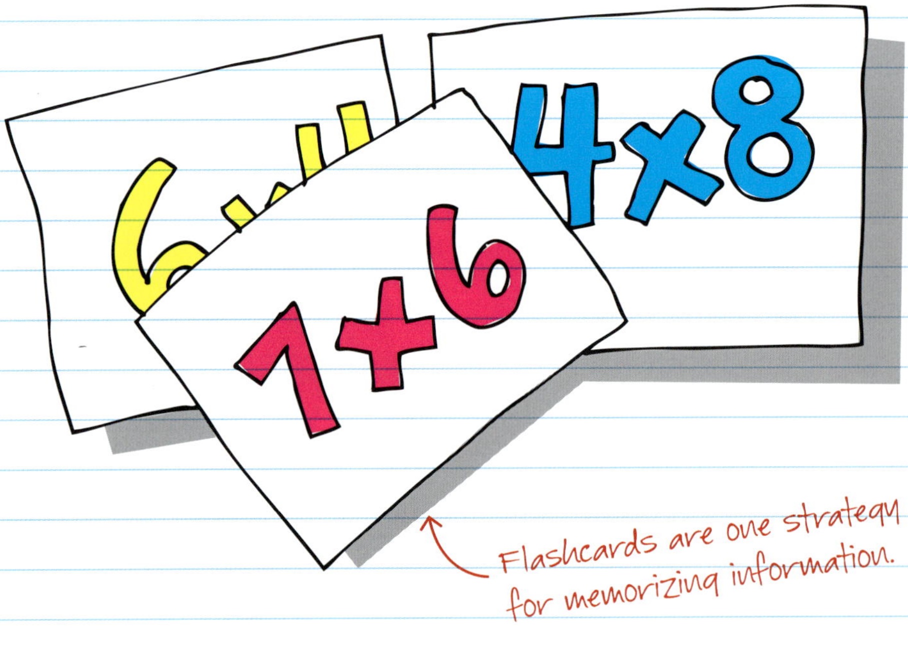

Flashcards are one strategy for memorizing information.

A portfolio can help you assess yourself. What is a portfolio? A portfolio is a collection of work kept over time. The items can include written work, photos, drawings, and even tests. You can also keep a digital portfolio with videos, podcasts, audio recordings, and computer files. The work may be stored in a folder, binder, or computer file. A portfolio is not a collection of all of your work. It is a collection of work you select to think and write about.

Keeping a portfolio for each school year can help you see how you have improved over time.

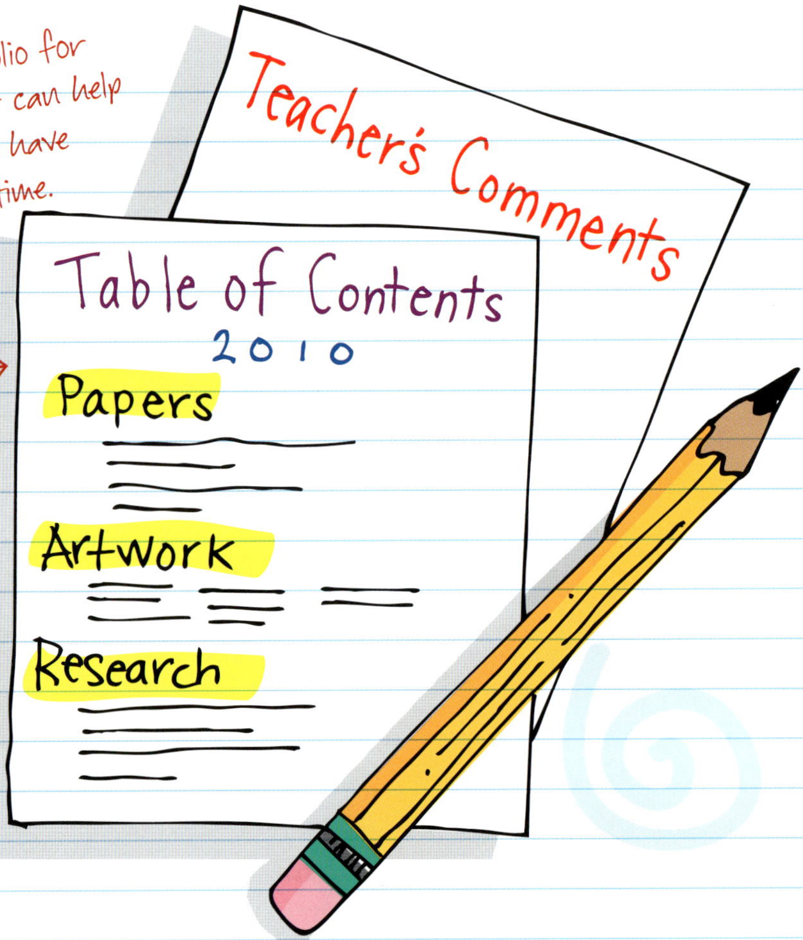

The portfolio should have a table of contents. It should also have a piece of reflective writing for each item you choose to include. Your teacher may ask you to write about why you chose a piece of work or why you think it is good. He or she may ask you to reflect on your goals for improvement. Keeping a portfolio from one year to the next helps you see how your work changes over time. It's like keeping a photo album of snapshots that show how you have grown from year to year. Portfolios are especially helpful for keeping track of your information skills.

CHAPTER FIVE

The Reviews Are In!

Every performer wants to please the audience. Clowns always hope for a laugh. Trapeze artists enjoy a round of applause. How about you? Are you the same when you wait for grades to be posted? Do you want to impress your teachers and family?

Performers hope for good reviews. Students do, too!

TRY THIS!

Do your parents keep all of your report cards? Ask to look at them. Examine your report cards from kindergarten through the most recent one you received. Can you spot any patterns? Do you always get A's in some classes?

continued →

TRY THIS! (CONTINUED)

Those subjects might be strengths. Are other classes always a struggle? Those subjects might be your weaknesses. You may need to work extra hard to do well in those classes. Do you get better grades during a certain time of year? If so, why might that be? Think about your answers. Who knew you could find out so much about yourself from some careful reflection?

Maybe reading is your area of strength, and managing deadlines your weakness. Try reading about how to become a better project manager.

Self-assessment is key to your success. When you evaluate your strengths and weaknesses, you set the groundwork for your own improvement. Do you have trouble meeting deadlines? Find ways to break every project down into smaller tasks that are easier to manage. Do you have a hard time keeping up with all the details of assignments? Learn to organize your notes. List which tasks you still need to finish. The trick is to spot challenges and find solutions that work for you.

Well, circus superstar? When you feel like you're about to fall off that high wire, don't be afraid to ask for help. Teachers and librarians are happy to offer advice for school success.

Take the tips you've learned and put them to use. Keep rating your progress and finding ways to improve. You're sure to run an organized show and get the glowing reviews you deserve . . . in the form of good grades!

If you need help, don't be afraid to ask. Teachers, librarians, and parents will be happy to help you succeed!

Glossary

bibliography **(bib-lee-OG-ruh-fee)** a list of writings about a subject or author or by one author

collaborate **(kuh-LAB-uh-rate)** to work together to do something

glossary **(GLOSS-uh-ree)** an alphabetical list of difficult words and their meanings in a book

index **(IN-dekss)** an alphabetical list of topics in a book with page numbers showing where they are found in the text

reliable sources **(ri-LYE-uh-buhl SOR-siz)** well-researched sources of information that are written by experts, have been reviewed by other experts in the field, and are usually current, depending on the topic

rubric **(ROO-brik)** a set of points, standards, or rules used to grade or evaluate something

search engine **(SURCH EN-juhn)** a tool used to find information on the World Wide Web

self-assessment **(self-uh-SESS-muhnt)** the process of rating your progress, strengths, and weaknesses and determining points that need improvement or changes you can make

table of contents **(TAY-buhl UHV KON-tentss)** a list found at the beginning of a book with chapter titles and the page numbers on which they begin

Find Out More

BOOKS

Orr, Tamra B. *Extraordinary Research Projects*. New York: Franklin Watts, 2006.

Somervill, Barbara A. *Team Projects*. Chicago: Heinemann Library, 2009.

Somervill, Barbara A. *Written Reports*. Chicago: Heinemann Library, 2009.

WEB SITES

BBC—Non-fiction

www.bbc.co.uk/schools/ks2bitesize/english/revision_bites/non_fiction.shtml

Learn more about different types of nonfiction resources.

KidsHealth—Group Projects for School

kidshealth.org/kid/feeling/school/group_projects.html

Find tips on collaborating and working well with others.

ReadWriteThink—Hints About Print

www.readwritethink.org/materials/hints-on-print/index.html

Follow an online tutorial on selecting nonfiction books and find a helpful evaluation guide.

Index

About the Author

Carol Gordon is an associate professor in the School of Communication and Information at Rutgers, The State University of New Jersey. She previously worked as a library media specialist at schools in Michigan, Massachusetts, Frankfurt, Germany, and London, England, and has served as head of the education library at Boston University.